ACADIA
NATIONAL PARK

BY KATHLEEN CONNORS

Gareth Stevens
PUBLISHING

Please visit our website, www.garethstevens.com. For a free color catalog of all our high-quality books, call toll free 1-800-542-2595 or fax 1-877-542-2596.

Library of Congress Cataloging-in-Publication Data

Connors, Kathleen.
Acadia National Park / by Kathleen Connors.
p. cm. — (Road trip: national parks)
Includes index.
ISBN 978-1-4824-1675-6 (pbk.)
ISBN 978-1-4824-1676-3 (6-pack)
ISBN 978-1-4824-1674-9 (library binding)
1. Acadia National Park (Me.) — Juvenile literature. 2. National parks and reserves — Juvenile literature. I. Connors, Kathleen. II. Title.
F27.M9 C66 2015
974.1—d23

First Edition

Published in 2016 by
Gareth Stevens Publishing
111 East 14th Street, Suite 349
New York, NY 10003

Copyright © 2016 Gareth Stevens Publishing

Designer: Andrea Davison-Bartolotta
Editor: Kristen Rajczak

Photo credits: Cover, p. 1 (left) Colin D. Young/Shutterstock.com; cover, pp. 1 (right), 5 (background), 11 (main), 12 Zack Frank/Shutterstock.com; cover, back cover, interior (background texture) Marilyn Volan/Shutterstock.com; pp. 4, 6, 8, 10, 12, 14, 16, 18, 20 (blue sign) Vitezslav Valka/Shutterstock.com; pp. 4, 6, 8, 10, 12, 14, 16, 18, 20, 21 (road) Renata Novackova/Shutterstock.com; p. 4 (main map) NPS.gov; p. 4 (inset map) Rainer Lesniewski/Shutterstock.com; p. 7 DeAgostini/Getty Images; p. 9 (map) United States General Land Office/LOC.gov; pp. 9 (background), 15 Doug Lemke/Shutterstock.com; p. 10 Harris & Erwing/LOC.gov; p. 11 (inset) Jerry Whaley/Shutterstock.com; p. 13 Robbie George/National Geographic/Getty Images; p. 14 Miro Vrlik Photography/Shutterstock.com; p. 16 Justin Lewis/The Image Bank/Getty Images; p. 17 Brian Swartz/iStock/Thinkstock; pp. 18, 19 (inset) Mark Daffey/Lonely Planet Images/ Getty Images; p. 19 (main) Tim Laman/National Geographic/Getty Images; p. 20 Jake Wyman/Aurora/Getty Images; p. 21 (notebook) 89studio/Shutterstock.com; p. 21 (map) Globe Turner, LLC/Getty Images.

Printed in the United States of America

CPSIA compliance information: Batch #CS16GS: For further information contact Gareth Stevens, New York, New York at 1-800-542-2595.

1037791

Contents

Words in the glossary appear in **bold** type the first time they are used in the text.

Island Park

Acadia National Park is a great place to visit. It's made up of towering mountains, steep cliffs, lovely meadows, and thick forests. In addition, it's surrounded by the thundering Atlantic Ocean. That's because the park is on an island!

In order to include Acadia National Park on a road trip, you have to cross a bridge from **mainland** Maine onto Mount Desert Island. The park takes up about 60 percent of the island's 108 square miles (280 sq km) as well as some land on nearby islands and the mainland.

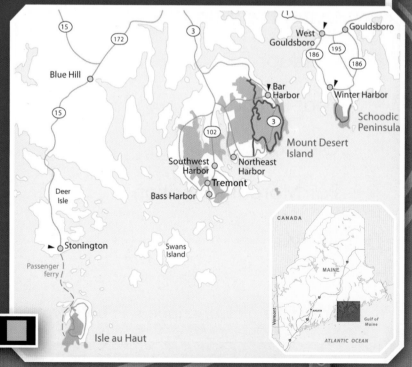

Acadia National Park

4

All About Acadia National Park

where found: Maine

year established: 1916 (as Sieur de Monts National Monument); 1919 (as Lafayette National Park); 1929 renamed Acadia National Park

size: 65 square miles (168 sq km)

number of visitors yearly: more than 2 million

common wildlife: eagles, loons, seals, frogs

common plant life: ferns, wildflowers, forests

major attractions: Cadillac Mountain, Bass Harbor Head Lighthouse, Sieur de Monts Spring

> Also found on Mount Desert Island are the towns of Bar Harbor, Mount Desert, Southwest Harbor, and Tremont.

The Wabanakis

About 5,000 years ago, a group of Native Americans called the Wabanakis made their homes on Mount Desert Island where Acadia National Park is today. They traveled to the island from the mainland in canoes made out of bark.

Europeans first came upon Mount Desert Island during the 1500s. By the 1800s, it was a common place for many people to visit—including Wabanakis. Though many lived on **reservations** elsewhere in Maine by then, the island was an important place to their people. This feeling continues today.

Pit Stop

The Wabanakis are made up of five Native American tribes: the Abenaki, Maliseet, Mi'kmaq, Passamaquoddy, and Penobscot.

The Mi'kmaq, shown in the image here, lived in eastern Canada, Maine, and Massachusetts.

7

Preserving the Land

During the 1880s, wealthy vacationers often visited Mount Desert Island. Many, including George B. Dorr, became interested in **preserving** the natural beauty of the island. In 1916, Dorr gave the US government the land he and others had **acquired** for preservation. It became a national monument!

Dorr continued to acquire land and worked to make the whole of it into a national park. In 1919, Lafayette National Park became the first national park created east of the Mississippi River. The name was changed to Acadia National Park in 1929.

Pit Stop

French explorers called parts of Maine and the present-day Canadian **provinces** of New Brunswick, Nova Scotia, Prince Edward Island, and Quebec "Acadia."

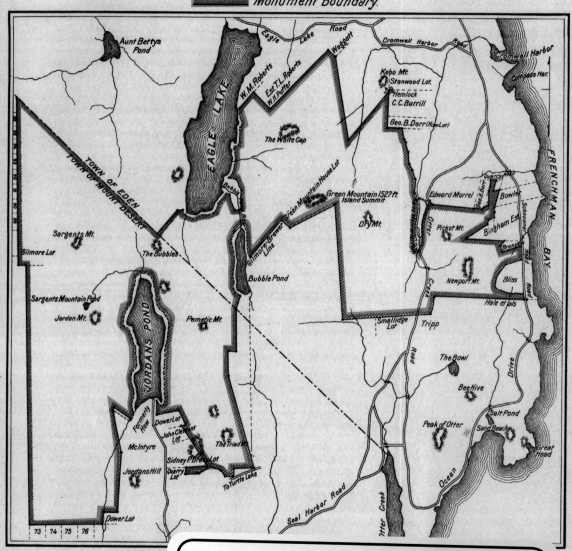

SIEUR de MONTS NATIONAL MONUMENT
Mount Desert Island
MAINE
Embracing the island summit and about five thousand acres of adjacent lands
Monument Boundary.

In 1916, Dorr's land was called Sieur de Monts National Monument after a spring found on the island. Both were named for Pierre du Guast (or du Gua), sieur de Monts.

Carriage Roads

Another wealthy vacationer to Mount Desert Island created one of the coolest features of Acadia National Park. John D. Rockefeller Jr. paid for and constructed broken-stone **carriage** roads between 1913 and 1940.

There are 45 miles (72 km) of carriage roads in Acadia National Park on which visitors can walk, bike, snowshoe, or cross-country ski. They're a great way to see lots of the park, especially since many of them show off beautiful **vistas** of the mountainous land and the ocean.

John D. Rockefeller Jr.

Pit Stop

Rockefeller also hired workers to use granite from the island to make 17 stone bridges.

carriage road

Rockefeller wanted to build roads that cars couldn't drive on so he could ride his horses in peace. Cars still aren't allowed on the carriage roads, though there is a road for cars around the park that's open from April to December.

Get Up There!

Do you like to get up early? It's worth getting up before the sun when visiting Acadia National Park. In the fall and winter, Cadillac Mountain is the first place on the East Coast that the sun touches as it rises. If you're not an early bird, the mountain's beauty is worth seeing anyway.

Cadillac Mountain is the highest point on the East Coast at 1,530 feet (466 m). Visitors can check out the sunrise—or just the view—after driving or hiking to the top.

Many visitors to Acadia National Park are there to see Cadillac Mountain.

Pit Stop

Even if you're heading to the top of Cadillac Mountain for a summer sunrise, it's going to be chilly up there! Bring a coat or blanket to enjoy the sight.

13

Lighting Dangerous Waters

Though it's surrounded by water, Mount Desert Island only has one lighthouse! The Bass Harbor Head Lighthouse was built in 1858 and is still working today. Its light flashes red to show passing ships the openings that lead to Blue Hill Bay and Bass Harbor.

Even so, many shipwrecks have happened around Mount Desert Island. In 2012, a group of park workers, **volunteers**, and scientists worked to uncover one wreck that was partly visible underwater. Who knows? You could be the next person to spot one!

You can visit the grounds of the lighthouse in Acadia National Park, but right now, only those operating the light can climb the steps to the lighthouse.

Pit Stop

Post

The Sieur de Monts Spring is another great spot to visit in the park. A **gazebo** was built over it in 1909, and today, the park's Nature Center and Wild Gardens are found near it.

Living the Wild Life

National parks are partly established to **protect** the plants and animals that live there. Acadia National Park is home to more than 1,000 kinds of plants. Ferns, such as rock polypody, grow in cool, shady spots. About 80 kinds of freshwater plants can be found in the lakes and streams of the park. Starflowers, lilies-of-the-valley, and other wildflowers dot the forests, too.

Acadia National Park is known for its birds! Eagles, peregrine falcons, and great blue herons, among many others, are often spotted.

Pit Stop

Moose and bears make their home in the park, too—but they're not spotted often.

Since the park is located on an island, **marine** animals are a big part of the wildlife seen when visiting the park. Seals can be seen in the water and laying on rocks.

Outdoor Fun

In addition to the great biking, hiking, and walking trails around Acadia National Park, there are bus and trolley tours. You can learn a lot about the wildlife and history of the park, as well as where some of the best views are!

Even though much of the park is forested, there's also the opportunity to go whale watching, sailing on a sunset cruise, or kayaking. Two beaches—one freshwater and one on the ocean—are good places to take a swim during the summer.

Pit Stop

One mountain in the park, Champlain Mountain, is known for a 1,000-foot (305 m) **sheer** rock face. It's a challenge for even experienced mountain climbers!

In order to continue caring for the park, it's important that all visitors clean up their trash and treat nature with respect.

visitors traveling around the park

Year-Round

Acadia National Park is found in the northeastern United States and has four seasons visitors should be prepared for!

Days during the spring and fall are commonly between 30°F and 70°F (−1°C and 21°C). Summer days may be as cool as 45°F (7°C) or as hot as 90°F (32°C)! Winters can be quite cold, usually ranging between 14°F and 35°F (−10°C and 2°C). No matter the time of year, there's something fun to do at Acadia National Park!

Pit Stop

Ice fishing, winter camping, and dogsledding are just some of the things winter visitors to Acadia National Park can do!

Road Trip Attractions

The Natural History Center
Learn more about the wildlife on Mount Desert Island.

Mount Desert Oceanarium
Learn more about lobsters and other marine life.

Bar Harbor

Abbe Museum
Find out about the Wabanaki tribe.

Mount Desert Land & Garden Preserve
Check out beautiful gardens and outlooks.

Acadia National Park

Glossary

acquire: to get as one's own

carriage: a wheeled vehicle often pulled by animals, such as horses

gazebo: a structure with a roof and open sides

mainland: a landmass or the main part of a landmass

marine: having to do with the sea

preserve: to keep something in its original state

protect: to keep safe

province: an area of a country

reservation: land set aside by the US government for Native Americans

sheer: having continuous steepness

vista: a distant view along a road

volunteer: a person who works without being paid

For More Information

Books

Graham, Amy. *Acadia National Park: Adventure, Explore, Discover.* Berkeley Heights, NJ: MyReportLinks.com Books, 2009.

Lindeen, Mary. *Parks of the U.S.A.* North Mankato, MN: Capstone Press, 2012.

Websites

For Kids—Acadia National Park
www.nps.gov/acad/forkids/index.htm
Check out the National Park Service's page for kids about exploring Acadia National Park.

NPF Kids
www.nationalparks.org/connect/npf-kids
Learn about more national parks to visit and what you can do at each one.

Index